BEAVERS

by Helen H. Moore

Illustrated by
Terri Talas

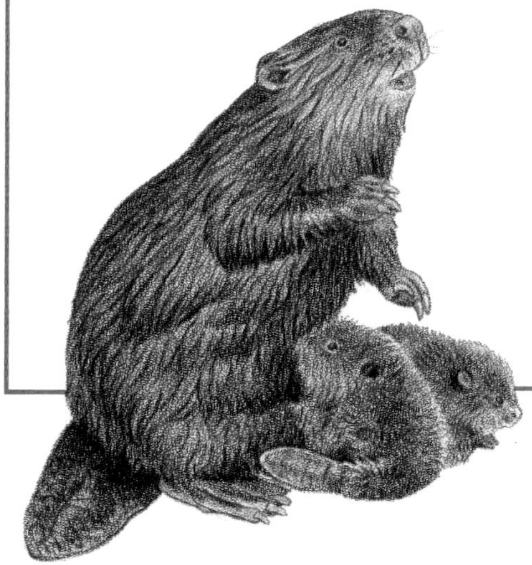

MONDO

To my "kits" Paul, Matt, and Mike, and their cousins Juno, Jack, and Max —H. H. M.

To the persevering nature and spirit of the beaver —T. T.

ACKNOWLEDGMENT: The publisher would like to thank Darrin Lunde, Department of Mammalogy, American Museum of Natural History, New York City, for his assistance in the preparation of this book.

Text copyright © 1996 by Helen H. Moore
Illustrations copyright © 1996 by Mondo Publishing

For information contact:
MONDO Publishing
980 Avenue of the Americas
New York, NY 10018

Printed in Hong Kong by South China Printing Co. (1988) Ltd.

01 02 03 04 05   9 8 7 6 5

Designed by Charlotte Staub
Production by The Kids at Our House

Library of Congress Cataloging-in-Publication Data
Moore, Helen H.
   Beavers / by Helen H. Moore ; illustrated by Terri Talas.
     p.   cm.
   Summary: Introduces the beaver, its characteristics, and its lifestyle.
   ISBN 1-57255-111-9 (pbk. : alk. paper). — ISBN 1-57255-112-7 (big book pbk. : alk. paper)
   1. Beavers—Juvenile literature. [1. Beavers.] I. Talas, Terri, ill. II. Title.
   QL737.R632M66   1996
   599.32'32—dc20   95-50295
                                                      CIP
                                                      AC

CONTENTS

gray squirrel

deer mouse

porcupine

4

WHAT IS A BEAVER?

Have you ever seen a porcupine, a gray squirrel, or a deer mouse? If you have, then you have seen one of the cousins of the beaver. But beavers themselves are hard to find because they usually live deep in the woods, hidden in small ponds.

beaver

The beaver belongs to the group of animals called mammals. All mammals have hair or fur on their bodies. Mammals also feed their babies milk from their own bodies.

monkey

human

beaver

dog

giraffe

whale

cat

Some of the many animals that are mammals.

hamster

The beaver is a special kind of mammal called a rodent. A rodent is a mammal that gnaws. This means the animal eats by taking many tiny bites with its very sharp front teeth.

deer mouse

gray squirrel

beaver

Some of the most commonly known rodents.

WHY DO BEAVERS GNAW?

Beavers gnaw to get food. They eat the bark, roots, and leaves of trees, but not the wood. Beavers are herbivores, or plant eaters, so they also like to eat berries, grass, and plants that grow in water.

Beavers also gnaw to cut down trees for food and to build dams. First they bite a tree trunk to make cuts in it. Then they gnaw the wood with their teeth. The beavers keep cutting and tearing away the trunk until the tree falls.

BUILDING DAMS

Beavers are safe in water, but they move very slowly on land. If beavers had to spend a lot of time away from water looking for food on land, they might get caught and eaten by predators.

wolf

coyote

lynx

Some of the beaver's worst enemies.

Most of the beavers' food grows on land, so they build dams to bring the water close to their food. Then they never have to be too far from the safety of water while they eat or gather branches, roots, and leaves.

A beaver dam can be more than 1000 feet (300 meters) long.

HOW A DAM IS BUILT

1. A slow-moving stream surrounded by trees is chosen as the spot for a beaver dam.

2. Brush and branches are gnawed from trees, dragged across the stream, and stuck into the mud at the bottom of the stream.

3. The dam is built up with logs, branches, and more sticks.

4. Mud and stones are pressed into cracks between the logs and branches to make the dam watertight.

beaver pond

stream

5. The finished dam is hard and strong. On one side is a new beaver pond. On the other side there is still a stream.

13

BUILDING LODGES

After beavers finish their dam they start building a lodge, or house. First the beavers build an island of sticks, rocks, and dry plants that will become the floor of the lodge.

lodge floor

The lodge floor rises above the water.

Next the beavers pile branches above the floor to form a dome-shaped roof. They pat mud against the branches to paste them together.

floor

tunnel

Beavers gnaw their way up from the bottom of the lodge to make tunnels.

16

roof

A hollow space is left between the floor and roof.

The lodge is now a pile of mud, sticks, and branches with no way to get in or out. So the beavers dig underwater tunnels. Finally the lodge is ready for a family of beavers.

17

BEAVER FAMILY LIFE

About six to eight beavers usually live together in one family. The family has a mother, a father, and some babies. Young beavers are called kits. A mother beaver has two to four kits every spring.

The beaver kits can walk and swim as soon as they are born. But they do not leave the lodge for a few weeks because they cannot dive down into the tunnel that leads to the outside.

Newborn kits cannot dive because they are too buoyant—they just float in water.

When the kits are older, they
like to play and wrestle with each
other. They take turns climbing up
to the top of the lodge and pushing
each other off into the water.

Maybe you have heard the saying "busy as a beaver." Beavers *do* work hard, but they like to have fun, too. In summer, they even go on vacation! They leave their lodge and swim upstream and downstream for miles.

21

When fall comes, the beavers prepare for winter. They fix their dams and lodges. They gather food and store it in the mud at the bottom of the pond. They may also pile stones on the food to keep it in place.

The cool water of the pond keeps the food fresh.

During winter, when the pond freezes over, the beavers swim underwater to their food pile, get food, and bring it back to the lodge. Staying underwater keeps the beavers safe from predators who look for them on the surface of the pond.

BEAVER FEATURES

How can beavers do all the amazing things they do? Nature has given beavers special tools to help them.

Teeth

A beaver's front teeth are called incisors. The incisors grow all during a beaver's life, but gnawing keeps them from getting too long.

The back edges of the incisors are softer than the front edges. The softer backs wear out faster, which gives the teeth a pointed, chisel shape.

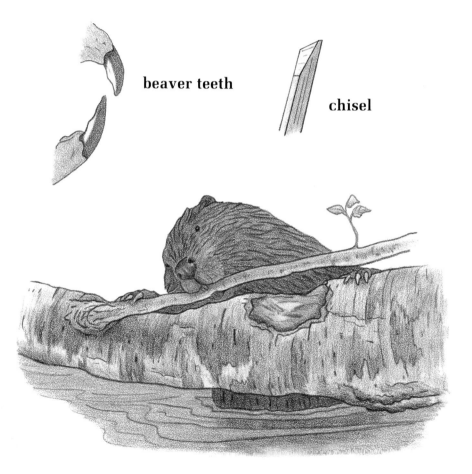

beaver teeth

chisel

A beaver's teeth are orange.

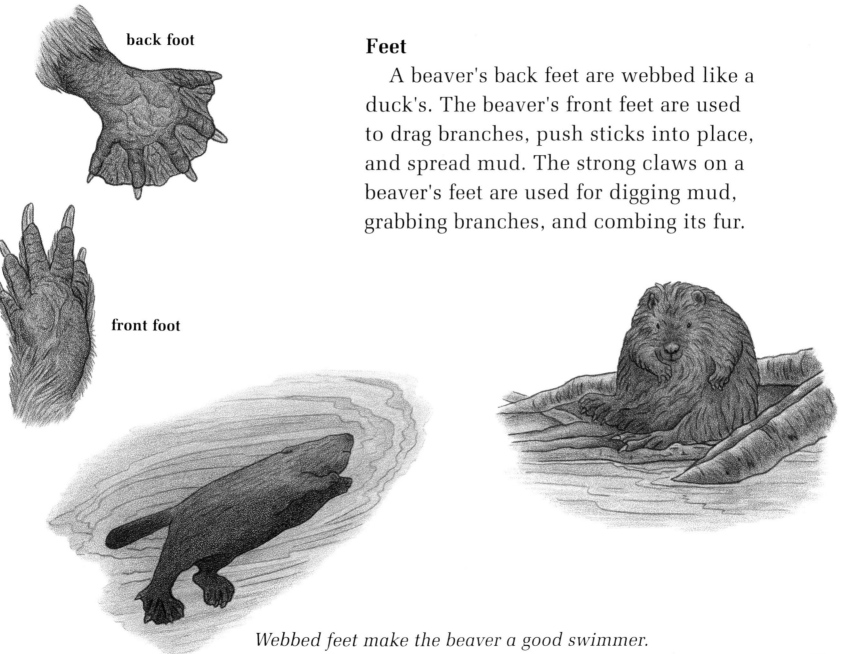

back foot

front foot

Feet

A beaver's back feet are webbed like a duck's. The beaver's front feet are used to drag branches, push sticks into place, and spread mud. The strong claws on a beaver's feet are used for digging mud, grabbing branches, and combing its fur.

Webbed feet make the beaver a good swimmer.

Tail

The beaver has a very unusual tail. It looks like a paddle, and it helps the beaver in many ways. A beaver can use its tail to smooth mud and to steer when it swims.

When a beaver senses that danger is near, it slaps its tail on the water or the ground. The slapping noise is a warning to other beavers. It tells them, "Danger! Back to the lodge!"

MORE ABOUT BEAVERS

Beavers can grow to be 3-4 feet (1-1¼ meters) long and weigh 70 pounds (32 kilograms). That's bigger than a first grader.

Beavers live to be about 12 years old.

Beavers can swim underwater for about 15 minutes without coming up for air.

Beavers say hello to each other
by nibbling each other's cheeks.

Beavers can tuck their cheeks
completely behind their front teeth
when they swim underwater. This
keeps water out of their mouths but
still allows them to gnaw.

Beavers get ticks in their fur from
living in wet, dark places. They
have a special comb-like claw that
helps them remove the ticks.

Beavers usually excrete their waste in water.
Some scientists think the waste makes the soil
at the bottom of the pond richer.

Glossary

brush a thick growth of small trees and shrubs

buoyant able to float in a liquid

chisel a tool with a sharp edge for cutting or
shaping wood, stone, or metal

dam a wall built across a stream or river to hold
back the flow of water

dome a rounded roof

excrete to pass waste matter from the body

flood to flow over onto nearby land

gnaw to wear away by taking many small
bites over and over

graze to feed on growing grass and other plants

herbivore an animal that feeds on plants

hollow having an empty space on the inside

incisor a sharp front tooth that has a cutting edge

island a piece of land surrounded by water

kit a young beaver

lodge the dome-shaped home of beavers, built of sticks and mud

mammal a warm-blooded animal with a backbone and hair or fur on its body; the female has glands that produce milk for its young

mound a heap or hill of earth, sand, or other material

newborn just born

paddle a flat, rounded object, often used to steer or push an animal forward in water

predator an animal that lives by killing and eating other animals

rodent an animal that has sharp front teeth for gnawing

surface the outside, top, or side of something

tick a tiny animal that sucks the blood of animals

watertight so tight that no water can get through

webbed having the toes joined by a piece of skin

INDEX